CHALK AND CHEESE AND CHATTER

(Digraphs)

1. Chalk and cheese and chatter,
Chalk and cheese and chatter,
Chalk and cheese and chatter
Are the ch, ch, ch, ch words I like to say.

2. Whip and whack and whistle,
Whip and whack and whistle,
Whip and whack and whistle
Are the wh, wh, wh, wh words I like to say.

3. Shoes and shine and shadow,
Shoes and shine and shadow,
Shoes and shine and shadow
Are the sh, sh, sh, sh words I like to say.

4. Phone and phrase and photo,
Phone and phrase and photo,
Phone and phrase and photo
Are the ph, ph, ph, ph words I like to say.

5. Thick and thief and thunder,
Thick and thief and thunder,
Thick and thief and thunder
Are the th, th, th, th words I like to say.

Teacher's Notes

- This is a fabulous song for embedding consonant digraphs. Write each digraph up on the whiteboard clearly so that the children can look at each one as they sing them. Once the children know the song really well, can they think of three different words beginning with 'ch' and sing those instead along to the backing track (CD track 22)? Try to do the same with the other verses.
- Five different consonant digraphs have been used for this song. Once the children are confident of these five, try using other consonant digraphs and coming up with your own lyrics. None of the words have to rhyme, so it's the perfect way to extend the song using the backing track (CD track 22).

WE'RE OFF TO RHYMING LAND

(Rhyming)

1. We're off to Rhyming Land,
We're going to find a goat,
And when we've found the goat,
We're going to find a boat.
A goat, a boat, we're off to Rhyming Land.

2. We're off to Rhyming Land,
We're going to find a mouse,
And when we've found the mouse,
We're going to find a house.
A mouse, a house, we're off to Rhyming Land.

3. We're off to Rhyming Land,
We're going to find a bear,
And when we've found the bear,
We're going to find a chair.
A bear, a chair, we're off to Rhyming Land.

4. We're off to Rhyming Land,
We're going to find a duck,
And when we've found the duck,
We're going to find a truck.
A duck, a truck, we're off to Rhyming Land.

5. We're off to Rhyming Land,
We're going to find a pig,
And when we've found the pig,
We're going to find a wig.
A pig, a wig, we're off to Rhyming Land.

Teacher's Notes

- A fantastic song for finding rhymes. Can the children find all the rhyming pairs? Then can they find other pairs of rhyming words with just one syllable? Sing along to the backing track (CD track 23) with the new lyrics that the children have come up with.
- Discuss what Rhyming Land might look like. Try creating a great big collage of Rhyming Land using the images that this song conjures up (e.g. a mouse in a house / a bear on a chair / a pig in a wig) and also the other lyrics that the children have come up with.

THE NIKI DAVIES BOOK OF

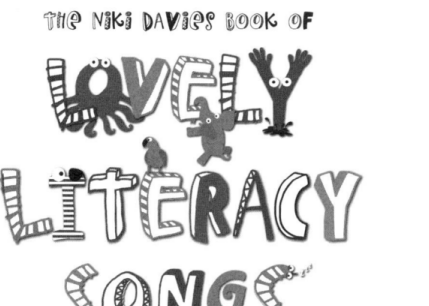

Tyssen Community School
Oldhill Street
London N16 6QA
Tel: 020 8806 4130
Fax: 020 8806 3620

	Page	CD Track (Vocal	Backing)
LYRICS & TEACHER'S NOTES	2	-	
THE SONGS			
Give Yourself A P-A-T On The Back	22	1	21
Chalk And Cheese And Chatter	24	2	22
We're Off To Rhyming Land	26	3	23
The Cricket And The Bat	28	4	24
Hey, Mr Pirate!	29	5	25
Big Elephants	32	6	26
I'm H, H, H, H, H, Huffed Out!	34	7	27
Once Upon A Time	36	8	28
Animal Dictionary	38	9	29
We're Going To Find The Octopus	41	10	30
Who Am I?	44	11	31
Whether The Weather	46	12	32
Lov-er-ly Mud	48	13	33
There Was A Young Parrot Called Pog	50	14	34
Wobble, Wobble Jellyfish	52	15	35
Doing-word Day	54	16	36
It's Great When You Know The Alphabet!	56	17	37
Books Are Amazing!	58	18	38
Sing A J-E-T	60	19	39
Big Ben	62	20	40

COPYRIGHT INFORMATION Inside back cover

© 2014 Out of the Ark Ltd

GIVE YOURSELF A P-A-T ON THE BACK

(Segmenting/blending letters)

1. Give yourself a p-a-t on the back,
A p-a-t on the back,
A p-a-t on the back,
Give yourself a **pat** on the back.

2. Put your hands on t-o-p of your head,
On t-o-p of your head,
On t-o-p of your head,
Put your hands on **top** of your head.

3. See if you can s-i-t on your hands,
S-i-t on your hands,
S-i-t on your hands,
See if you can **sit** on your hands.

4. Do a little t-a-p on your knees,
A t-a-p on your knees,
A t-a-p on your knees,
Do a little **tap** on your knees.

5. Can you count to t-e-n? Yes you can.
To t-e-n? Yes you can.
To t-e-n? Yes you can.
Can you count to **ten**? Yes I can.

One, two, three, four, five, six, seven, eight, nine, ten!

6. Give yourself a p-a-t on the back,
A p-a-t on the back,
A p-a-t on the back,
Give yourself a **pat** on the back.

Teacher's Notes

- Write the words up clearly on the whiteboard before the children start to sing this song so that they can see each sound as they sing it.
- Add the actions to the song, encouraging the children to make sure they sing at the same time! It might help to do a little pat/tap on each of the three letters that you sing for those verses instead of lots of pats/taps.

(Homographs)

1. Hey, little cricket,
Do you like playing cricket?
If you're a little cricket
Then it's cricket you shall play.

2. Here comes the bat and he says
He wants to bat now,
He wants the bat to bat with
So just give the bat the bat.

3. Then the bat and the cricket,
Off they went playing cricket,
The cricket had the cricket ball,
The bat just had his bat.

Teacher's Notes

- This song conjures up lots of funny pictures! Ask the children to try to draw a bat and a cricket playing cricket to help them to remember their homographs.
- There are lots of other animal homographs (duck, badger, fox, rabbit etc.) and homophones (bee, hare, whale, moose, horse, deer etc.). Have fun discovering these and chatting about the difference between homographs and homophones.

(Creative writing)

1. Hey, Mr Pirate with your big black hat,
Sailing over the sea,
Hey, Mr Pirate with your big black hat,
Are you looking for me? Well!

CHORUS You can't have my treasure!
I'm not scared of you.
Turn around and off you go,
You can't have my treasure!

2. Hey, Mr Pirate with your black eyepatch,
And your galleon fine,
Hey, Mr Pirate with your black eyepatch,
All this treasure is mine, so...

CHORUS

3. Hey, Mr Pirate with your shiny hook
Flashing there in the sun,
Hey, Mr Pirate with your shiny hook,
I'll be stopping your fun, 'cos...

CHORUS

4. Hey, Mr Pirate with your parrot pal,
You can never catch me,
Hey, Mr Pirate with your parrot pal,
You will very soon see that...

CHORUS

Teacher's Notes

- A fabulous song for sparking the children's imaginations for creative writing. Using the song as a basis, write a story all about the pirate. Where has he come from? Whose treasure is he trying to steal? Can you give the characters names and describe how they look? Finally, try to draw a picture of the pirate using the hat, the eyepatch, the hook and the parrot from the song. Can you draw the other characters in your story?
- Split the children into small groups and assign each group a commonly used letter of the alphabet. Ask the children to come up with a set of adjectives starting with that letter to describe a pirate (e.g. M for mean, menacing and money-grabbing pirates / S for silly, scary and selfish pirates).

(Acronyms)

1. **B**ig **e**lephants **c**an't **a**dd **u**p **s**ums **e**asily,
Big **e**lephants **c**an't **a**dd **u**p **s**ums **e**asily
Because, because
It gets them in a tiz woz,
Big **e**lephants **c**an't **a**dd **u**p **s**ums **e**asily.

2. **L**ennie **A**nt's **u**ncle **g**ot **h**iccups **e**very **d**ay,
Lennie **A**nt's **u**ncle **g**ot **h**iccups **e**very **d**ay
And he **laughed**, he **laughed**,
Because they made him talk fast,
Lennie **A**nt's **u**ncle **g**ot **h**iccups **e**very **d**ay.

3. **T**en **h**appy **o**wls **u**p **g**reat **h**ollow **t**rees,
Ten **h**appy **o**wls **u**p **g**reat **h**ollow **t**rees,
They **thought**, they **thought**
That they could have a nice talk,
Ten **h**appy **o**wls **u**p **g**reat **h**ollow **t**rees.

4. **F**reddie **R**at **i**s **e**agerly **n**ibbling **d**andelions,
Freddie **R**at **i**s **e**agerly **n**ibbling **d**andelions
With his **friend**, his **friend**,
They're eating dandelions again,
Freddie **R**at **i**s **e**agerly **n**ibbling **d**andelions.

Teacher's Notes

- Because, laughed, thought and friend – four really tricky spelling words learnt quickly in one song through fun acronyms! Encourage the children just to say the words to this song before singing them so that they're confident of the lyrics and recognise that they sing the spelt-out word of the first two lines on the third line of the song. It would be really helpful to have each of the four words written up on the whiteboard so that they can see the pattern well.

- Illustrating each verse of the song will help to cement each acronym in the children's memories. Divide a piece of paper into four boxes and get the children to draw a picture to depict each verse and write the spelling word clearly at the top of each box.

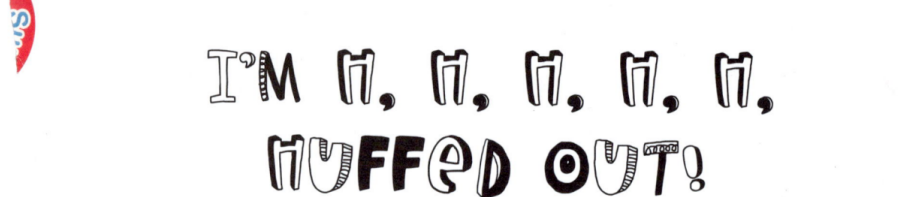

(Phonemes)

1. I'm h, h, h, h, h, huffed out,
I'm h, h, h, h, h, huffed out,
I'm going up a h, h, h, h, hill
And I'm huffed out!

2. I've g, g, g, got to the top,
I've g, g, g, got to the top,
It's v, v, v, v, very hot,
I'm at the top!

3. But now it's w, w, windy,
But now it's w, w, windy,
I'm feeling c, c, c, c, cold,
It's w, w, w, w, windy!

4. I'm f, f, f, f, freezing,
I'm f, f, f, f, freezing,
It's not f, f, f, funny
'Cos I'm f, f, f, f, freezing!

5. I'm s, s, s, s, sneezing,
I'm s, s, s, s, sneezing,
It's s, s, s, s, stormy
And I'm s, s, s, s, sneezing!

6. I'm d, d, d, d, dashing down,
I'm d, d, d, d, dashing down,
I want to be d, d, d, down,
I'm dashing down!

7. I'm h, h, h, h, h, huffed out,
I'm h, h, h, h, h, huffed out,
I'm down the h, h, h, h, hill
And I'm huffed out!

Teacher's Notes

* A great song for practising different letter sounds. Point out the 'accelerando' in verse 6 where the music gets quicker and the 'rall' just before verse 7 as the music slows down.

ONCE UPON A TIME

(Story formula; creative writing)

1. Once upon a time there was a robber,
He had a big bag of loot.
Along came the police car as fast as he could,
The robber was caught and all was good.
The end.

2. Once upon a time there was a fire,
Inside a little house.
Along came the fire engine, fast as he could,
The fire was put out and all was good.
The end.

3. Once upon a time there was a lady,
Who one day felt quite ill.
Along came the ambulance as fast as he could,
He took her to hospital and all was good.
The end.

4. Once upon a time there was a toy shop,
It ran right out of toys.
Along came the lorry as fast as he could,
The shop was stocked up again and all was good.
The end.

5. Once upon a time there was a donkey,
Who got stuck on a hill.
Along came the helicopter, fast as he could,
The donkey was saved and all was good.
The end.

Teacher's Notes

- A great song for introducing the Once Upon A Time story formula, establishing a main character or thing, creating a problem, finding a solution and giving an ending. Once the children are familiar with the song, ask them to come up with their own character, problem, solution and ending in just a few short lines.

- Try using this song as a way to extend creative writing by using each verse as a basic story structure. Give one of the verses to each child. Ask them to write each line of the song down and extend it (e.g. 'Once upon a time there was a robber' – what did the robber look like? What sort of person was he? 'He had a big bag of loot' – what was in the bag and where had he stolen it from? etc.).

ANIMAL DICTIONARY

(Dictionary; alphabet)

CHORUS Look up a word, look up a word,
Look up a word with me.
You can find all sorts of words
In the dictionary.

1 There's A for ant, B for bear, C can be for crab,
D for dog, E for eel, F for frog on a lily pad,
G for goat, H for hen, I for iguana,
J for jellyfish, K for koala, L for lovely llama.

CHORUS

2 There's M for moth, N for newt, O for octopus,
P for panda, Q for quail, R must be for rhinoceros,
S for snake, T for toad, U for spiky urchin,
V for vulture, W's wallaby, X for x-ray fish in the sea,
Y for yak, aren't we clever?
And finally Z for zebra!

Teacher's Notes

- This is a fantastic song for introducing children to the dictionary. The song uses animals for each letter. Can the children choose different subjects and try to find a word beginning with each letter of the alphabet (e.g. foods; children's names; countries)?

- This song would make a great animal dictionary mural. Give each child the same-sized piece of plain paper and assign a letter to each of them. Ask them to draw the letter in the corner of the paper and then draw the corresponding animal for that letter using the rest of the sheet of the paper. Encourage them to use bold colours and black outlines so that when they are all hung next to each other on the wall, they can be seen well from a distance.

WE'RE GOING TO FIND THE OCTOPUS

(Onomatopoeia; creative writing)

CHORUS We're going to find the octopus,
We're going to find the octopus,
We're going to find the octopus
In the sea.

1. What's that sound? Ripple, ripple.
What's that sound? Ripple, ripple.
It's just a fish who's having fun,
So keep on looking everyone. **CHORUS**

2. What's that sound? Splash, splash.
What's that sound? Splash, splash.
It's just a turtle having fun,
So keep on looking everyone. **CHORUS**

3. What's that sound? Swoosh, swoosh.
What's that sound? Swoosh, swoosh.
It's just a dolphin having fun,
So keep on looking everyone. **CHORUS**

4. What's that sound? Spray, spray.
What's that sound? Spray, spray.
It's just a whale who's having fun,
So keep on looking everyone. **CHORUS**

5. What's that sound? Splish, splish.
What's that sound? Splish, splish.
It's just a seahorse having fun,
So keep on looking everyone. **CHORUS**

6. What's that sound? Bubble, bubble.
What's that sound? Bubble, bubble.
The octopus is having fun,
So come and see him everyone.

LAST CHORUS We're swimming with the octopus,
We're swimming with the octopus,
We're swimming with the octopus
In the sea.

Teacher's Notes

- Have fun filling this song with lots of actions and percussion!

(Fairytale characters; storytelling)

1. I have a red cloak, I have a red hood,
Who am I?
My grandma lives in a deep, dark wood,
Who am I?
Red Riding Hood.

2. I climbed a big beanstalk, there and back,
Who am I?
I cut it down with a great big axe,
Who am I?
My name is Jack.

3. We're clever and pink and not so big,
Who are we?
We stopped the wolf and his wicked tricks,
Who are we?
The three little pigs.

4. I'm grumpy and ugly, so I'm told,
Who am I?
I'd like to eat a billy goat up whole,
Who am I?
The big bad troll.

5. You couldn't catch me, I ran and ran,
Who am I?
I met a fox with a clever plan,
Who am I?
The gingerbread man.

Teacher's Notes

- Make some mini-books based on your favourite fairytale story. Draw pictures to illustrate the story and design a beautiful front cover with a bold title.
- Split the children into five groups, assign them each a character from the five verses and have a mask-making session. Each group can put on their masks for their verse while the rest of the groups sing.
- Invite another class in and sing the song nice and clearly so that they can hear the words well. Stop the CD after the last 'Who am I?' of each verse and see if they can guess which fairytale character the children are singing about.

(Homophones)

1 Whether the weather is cold,
Or whether the weather is hot,
Whatever the weather it won't be forever,
It's just the weather we've got.

2 Whether the weather is fine,
Or whether the weather is not,
Whatever the weather it won't be forever,
It's just the weather we've got.

3 Whether the weather is cold,
Or whether the weather is hot,
Whatever the weather it won't be forever,
It's just the weather we've got.

Teacher's Notes

- Explore some other homophones and have a go at writing a short poem or story using them. Here are some title ideas: 'The Hare with the Auburn Hair'; 'Which Witch is Which?'; 'The Pair of Pear Trees'; 'My Journey to See the Sea'.
- With the children, create a large pear tree to display on the classroom wall. Use paints, collage, paper mosaic or any other media you like. Fill the tree with lots of pairs of pears and write homophones in each.

(Onomatopoeia; adjectives)

1. Squishy, squashy, oh lov-er-ly mud,
   Bubbly, squidgy, glug, glug, glug,
   Sticky, yucky, mucky mud,
   Oh, what do I like?
   Lov-er-ly mud!

2. Slippy, sloppy, oh lov-er-ly mud,
   Oozy, Woozy, glug, glug, glug,
   Sticky, yucky, mucky mud,
   Oh, what do I like?
   Lov-er-ly mud!

3. Slimy, squirty, oh lov-er-ly mud,
   Goopy, gloopy, glug, glug, glug,
   Sticky, yucky, mucky mud,
   Oh, what do I like?
   Lov-er-ly mud!

4. Squishy, squashy, oh lov-er-ly mud,
   Bubbly, squidgy, glug, glug, glug,
   Sticky, yucky, mucky mud,
   Oh, what do I like?
   Lov-er-ly mud!

Teacher's Notes

- Listen to the children singing on the CD and try to copy the way that they sing each onomatopoeia, emphasising them and trying to imagine the mud as they sing.
- Obviously 'lov-er-ly' is spelt incorrectly in this song so that it can be split into three syllables and sung over three notes. In some parts of Britain lovely is pronounced using 3 syllables, like the song, whereas in other parts it's spoken over two syllables. Talk about different accents and different pronunciations of words. Do any of the children have a family member who pronounces certain words differently to them?
- Hippos love to roll around in mud. Ask the children to draw a hippo in a great muddy swamp and write all the adjectives in the song around the picture in different colours. Search for Flanders and Swann's fabulous Hippopotamus Song to play as the children draw.

(Poetry; limerick)

1. There was a young parrot called Pog
Who thought he was really a dog,
He'd fly to the roof
With a very loud woof
And wag all his feathers a lot.

2. There was an old lady from Wales
Whose favourite supper was snails,
She ate them with cheese
And they slid down with ease
Just leaving their silvery trails.

3. There was an old goblin from Leeds
Who had terribly knobbly knees,
He said, 'When I chatter,
My knees they go clatter
And it's even worse when I sneeze!'

4. There was a young fellow called Bob
Who had a peculiar job,
He went in his wagon
To go and find dragons
And fought them with corn on the cob.

Teacher's Notes

- Can the children write their own limerick? The easiest way to start is to think of three words that rhyme to form the last words of lines 1, 2 and 5. Then find a pair of rhyming words for the last words of lines 3 and 4. Limericks are nonsense rhymes and therefore once you have your rhyming words, you can pretty much write anything infront of them – the dafter the better!
- Ask the children to come up with some nonsense words to help them to remember the rhythm of a limerick, e.g. 'Dee diddly, diddly plonk / dee diddly, diddly plonk / dee diddly, diddly, diddly dee / dee diddly, diddly plonk!'

(Compound words)

1. Wobble, wobble **jelly**, funny **fish**,
Your tentacles all going swish.
Wobble, wobble jelly, funny fish,
You're a **jellyfish**.

2. See the little **dragon**, watch him **fly**,
He's green and gold and flying high.
See the little dragon, watch him fly,
He's a **dragonfly**.

3. Hear the rushing **water**, see it **fall**,
It comes down from the mountain tall.
Hear the rushing water, see it fall,
It's a **waterfall**.

4. If you're feeling **sleepy**, rest your **head**,
Just lie down in a cosy bed.
If you're feeling sleepy, rest your head,
You're a **sleepyhead**.

Teacher's Notes

- Play a game of pairs where various words (that make up compound words) are written on cards and turned upside-down. Turn up two cards at a time, looking for the compound-word combinations. Along with those in the song, here are some more word suggestions to include: butter/fly; arm/pit; foot/ball; hair/cut; rattle/snake; humming/bird; pepper/mint; sun/flower; moon/light.
- For some compound words, it is very obvious why the two words have been put together to make another word, e.g. haircut, hummingbird, waterfall. Others are not so obvious. Discuss why dragonfly, butterfly, peppermint etc. may have been given those names.

DOING-WORD DAY

(Verbs)

1. I'm running, I'm dashing, I'm running round and round,
I'm jumping, I'm bouncing on and off the ground.
There's so much I can do and this is what I'm doing
Because it is a doing-word day.

2. I'm marching, I'm stomping, I'm marching up and down,
I'm marching, I'm stomping, with a stamping sound.
There's so much I can do and this is what I'm doing
Because it is a doing-word day.

3. I'm crawling, I'm creeping, I'm crawling very slow,
I'm crawling, I'm creeping, keeping very low.
There's so much I can do and this is what I'm doing
Because it is a doing-word day.

4. I'm flying, I'm gliding, I'm flying like a plane,
I'm flying, I'm gliding, flying back again.
There's so much I can do and this is what I'm doing
Because it is a doing-word day.

Teacher's Notes

- A great song to act out as you sing!
- Listen to the backing track of this song with the children (CD track 36). Can they hear the different instruments that have been used for each verse to illustrate the different verbs? Can they hear the marching snare drum and piccolo in verse 2 and the stringed instruments in verses 3 and 4, giving them a smoother feel to describe crawling, creeping, flying and gliding?
- Have a look through your percussion box and ask the children to choose an instrument and decide which verse of the song they could play it for (e.g. shakers/tambourines for verse 1; drums/woodblocks for verse 2; rainsticks/glissandos on glocks for verse 3; guiros for verse 4).

(Alphabet)

A, B, C, D, E, F, G,
Come and sing the alphabet with me,
H, I, J, K, L, M, N,
When we've finished we'll start again,
O, P, Q, R, S, T, U,
We can do it, me and you,
V, W, X, Y, Z,
It's great when you know the alphabet!

Repeat whole song

Teacher's Notes

- Give each child a piece of A4 card and assign them a letter of the alphabet. Get them to draw and decorate their letter on the card, making it as big as they can to fill the whole space. (Depending on the number of children in your class you may have more than one child per letter or a few children with two letters each.) Once all your cards have been created, sing through the song and ask each child to stand and then sit quickly as their letter is sung, holding up their card infront of them. This should be great fun and is also a good activity for those children who may not find it that easy to sing through the song themselves yet.
- Using a selection of percussion instruments, experiment with playing on different beats of the bar. Start by explaining that there are 4 beats in each bar in this song. Can the children count them as the music plays? When they've mastered this, ask them to pick up their percussion instrument and play it only on the first beat of each bar. You could extend the exercise to play on the stronger beats of the bar (beats 1 and 3); all the off-beats (beats 2 and 4); or sit in a circle and take it in turns to play on consecutive beats as the music plays.

(Information books)

1. Books are amazing, books are fun,
Books are here for everyone.
You can find out all about anything,
Rockets in space, snowflake shapes,
You can find out anything.

2. Books are amazing, books are fun,
Books are here for everyone.
You can find out all about anything,
Tractors and cranes, big steam trains,
You can find out anything.

3. Books are amazing, books are fun,
Books are here for everyone.
You can find out all about anything,
How do birds fly? What's in the sky?
You can find out anything.

4. Books are amazing, books are fun,
Books are here for everyone.
You can find out all about anything,
Butterfly wings, queens and kings,
You can find out anything.

5. Books are amazing, books are fun,
Books are here for everyone.
You can find out all about anything,
Racing cars, the moon and stars,
You can find out anything.

Teacher's Notes

- Ideal for use in a themed assembly, during Book Week, or to head up any literacy topic, this lively song will also inspire the children to dip into some information books.
- Do any of the children have an information book about any of the subjects mentioned in the song?
- Make your own information books. Staple together four pieces of A5 paper. Ask the children to think of one thing that they know quite a lot about (e.g. how to play football; looking after a pet; playing a musical instrument; trees; healthy food). Think of six facts about each subject, write each one on a different page of your book and illustrate them. Can the children design an exciting front cover with a title for their book and their name?

(Segmenting/blending letters)

1. Sing a j-e-t, sing a j-e-t, sing a j-e-t,
Can you sing a jet?
Sing a j-e-t, sing a j-e-t, sing a j-e-t,
Can you sing a jet?

2. Sing a p-i-g, sing a p-i-g, sing a p-i-g,
Can you sing a pig?
Sing a p-i-g, sing a p-i-g, sing a p-i-g,
Can you sing a pig?

3. Sing a b-u-s, sing a b-u-s, sing a b-u-s,
Can you sing a bus?
Sing a b-u-s, sing a b-u-s, sing a b-u-s,
Can you sing a bus?

4. Sing a f-o-x, sing a f-o-x, sing a f-o-x,
Can you sing a fox?
Sing a f-o-x, sing a f-o-x, sing a f-o-x,
Can you sing a fox?

5. Sing a v-a-n, sing a v-a-n, sing a v-a-n,
Can you sing a van?
Sing a v-a-n, sing a v-a-n, sing a v-a-n,
Can you sing a van?

Teacher's Notes

- Write the words up clearly on a whiteboard before singing this so that the children can see each letter sound as they sing through it. How many letters are in the alphabet? How many different letters are contained within the song? How many letters have not been included?

- This is a great song for including the children's own three-letter words as there are no rhymes and therefore any three-letter word can be included. Try to find words that include at least one letter that hasn't already been used through the song. Depending on the level of your children, you could begin to include some words using consonant digraphs (th, ch, sh, etc.).

(Onomatopoeia; alliteration)

1. Tick, tock, tick, tock,
   The great big pendulum's swinging,
   Tick, tock, tick, tock,
   The great big pendulum swings.

2. Clitter, clatter, clunk, clitter, clatter, clunk,
   The gears and the wheels are turning,
   Clitter, clatter, clunk, clitter, clatter, clunk,
   The gears and the wheels turn round.

3. Ding, dang, dong, ding, dang, dong,
   The chimes are ringing, ringing,
   Ding, dang, dong, ding, dang, dong,
   The chimes are ringing their tune.

4. Boom, bong, boom, bong,
   The great big bell is ringing,
   Boom, bong, boom, bong,
   The great big, wonderful bell.

Teacher's Notes

- Put out a selection of percussion instruments in the classroom and ask the children to select instruments that they think represent the clock sounds in each of the verses. Using these instruments, have some fun playing along to the song. For each verse, try to play the rhythm that you hear sung in the first line of lyrics.
- For this song we have used lots of onomatopoeic words that relate to the sounds that a clock makes. Can the children think of some other household objects that make noises? What onomatopoeic words can they find to describe the noises?

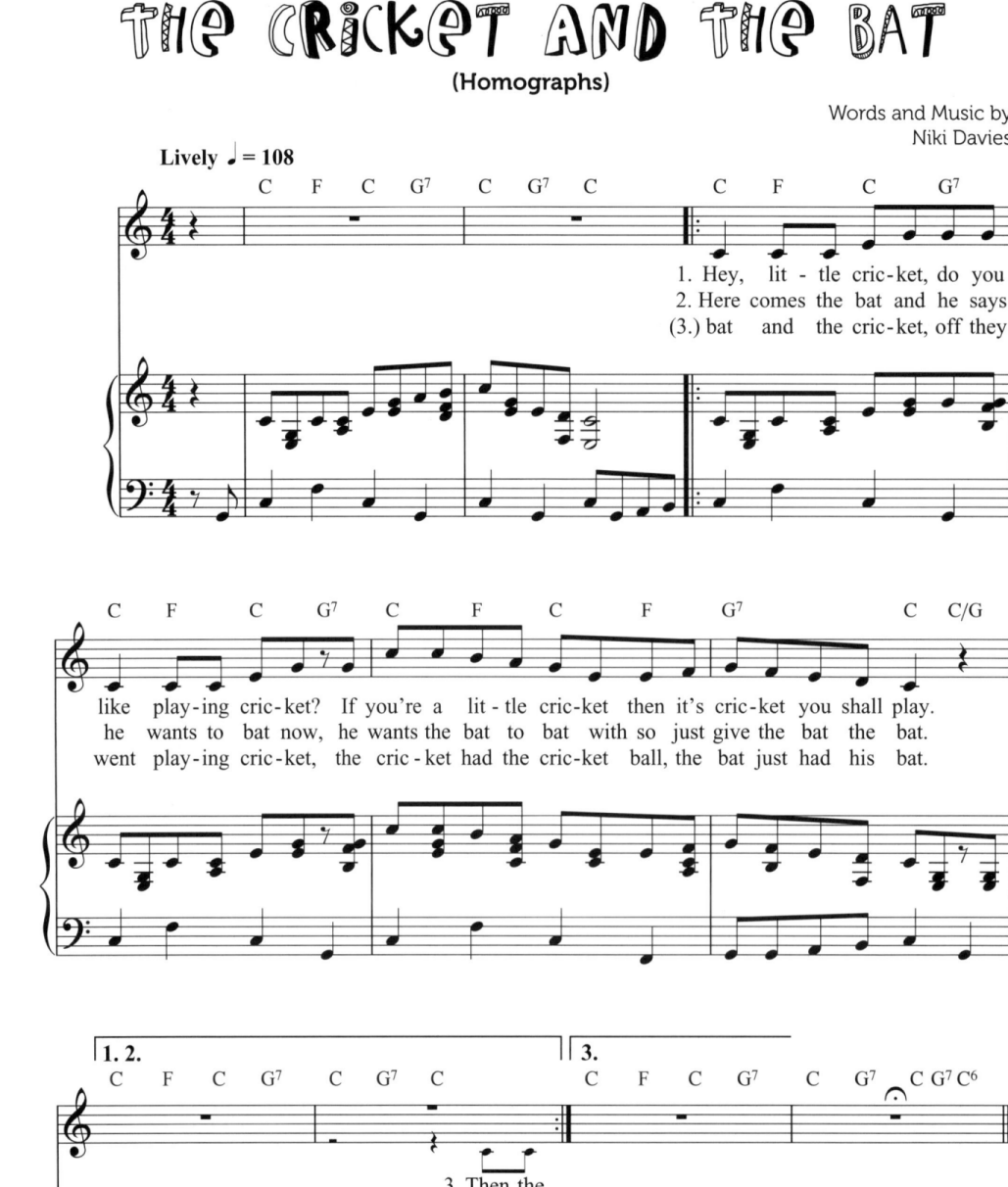

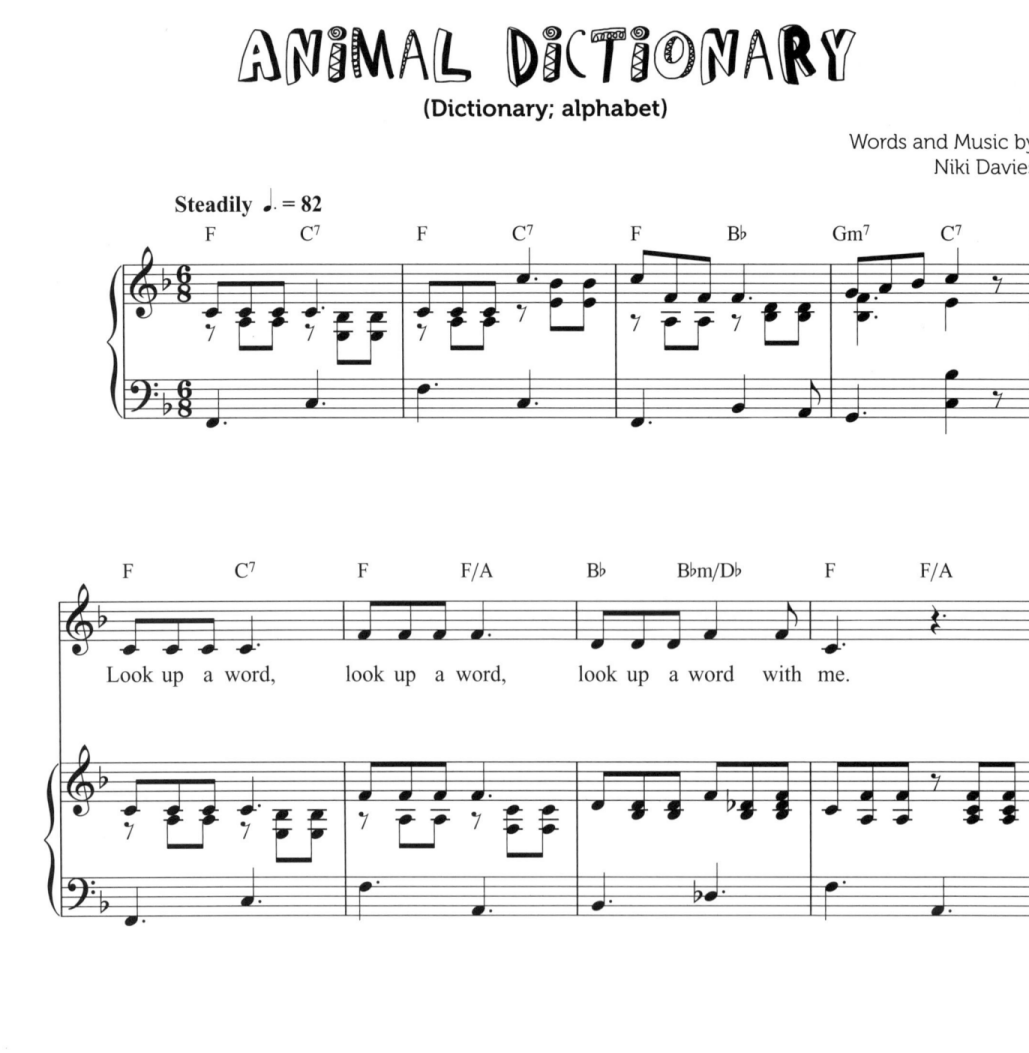

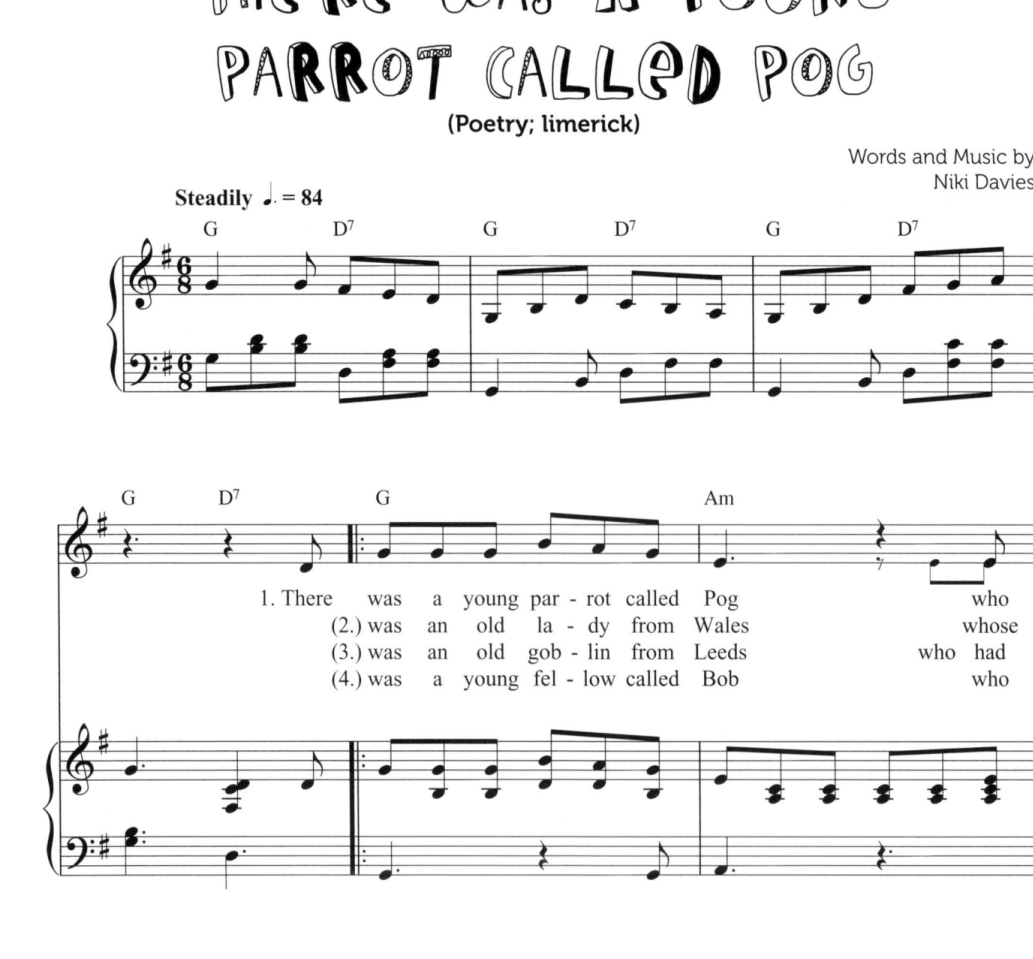